D0553017

zen BY THE BRUSH
A Japanese Painting and Meditation Set

Myochi Nancy O'Hara
Illustrations by Seiko Susan Morningstar

FALL RIVER PRESS

This 2009 edition published by Fall River Press,
by arrangement with becker&mayer!

Produced by becker&mayer!, Bellevue, Washington
www.beckermayer.com

Editorial: Ben Raker
Design: Joanna Price
Production coordination: Cindy Lashley
Project management: Sheila Kamuda

Fall River Press
122 Fifth Avenue
New York, NY 10011

ISBN-13: 978-1-4351-1179-0

Printed and bound in China

10 9 8 7 6 5 4 3 2 1

Calm yourself with breath—
Dip the brush, hold gently, draw.
Whatever comes, comes.

MYOCHI

EVER SINCE a human first etched a drawing onto a stone wall and created a written language, we have been using art to communicate our understanding of the mysteries of life. For centuries, Zen monks in Japan have utilized the ancient traditions of calligraphy, ink painting, and poetry to aid them in meditation and to express their insights. After a period of meditation, artistic activities further calm the body and mind and offer another way to tap into one's intuitive nature. Like meditation, these practices have spread to the West and are being employed by monks and laypeople alike to deepen their spiritual experiences.

In Zen, true understanding is believed to be beyond words, beyond thought, as demonstrated in one of Buddha's famous teachings when he held up a flower in his hand and said nothing. Simple and direct, this wordless gesture enlightened one of his students. Zen practice invites us to transcend our ego and wake up to the true nature of all things.

In Zen brush art, as in meditation, the breath and the present moment are the foundation for practice. A character or a line is written once and never altered in any way. Think of it this way: one line, one breath. Just as we cannot go back and change the nature of the breath we just took, there is no need to go back and change anything about our art. Simply take another breath; draw another line.

The painting board and brush in this kit will facilitate the practice of non-attachment, an important part of Zen philosophy. The process is simple: Dip the brush in water, paint an image on the board, and watch it fade as the board dries. Then paint something else. The impermanence of the image will deepen your appreciation and understanding of the impermanent nature of all things. Paying attention to your breath as you paint will promote relaxation, encourage harmony between body and mind, and create a peaceful, happy spirit. Use the painting as a meditation. Notice the dualistic judgment that arises as you paint. If you judge something you've painted as good or bad, or if you've brought into the moment of painting a disturbing emotion, such as anger or frustration, breathe it away as you watch the image fade.

Traditionally, Zen art is done while kneeling with the painting surface flat on the floor. Give this technique a try, but sitting at a desk or table with the painting board flat will work as well (the board's fold-out easel should be used to prop up the image after painting). Begin by holding the brush lightly between thumb and forefinger, perpendicular to the board. This will allow you to use your whole arm and body in the process. Experiment with the amount of water. The wetter the brush and the stronger the pressure, the thicker the line and the longer it lasts. Develop your own painting style as you go. There are no set rules about how an image should look or how many brush strokes one should make; in Zen, one is often encouraged to learn by doing—instruction is kept to a minimum. Play with your brush strokes: left to right, right to left, etc. Relax!

This book provides meditative verses and images for inspiration. Begin each painting session with a period of silent meditation. Then, when ready, choose an image or a saying from anywhere in the book that appeals to you in that moment. Read the passage and then replicate the image. Don't be concerned about exact duplication. The point is to create your own expressive images, not to copy every bird, branch, and flower. Think of the quote as you paint. Or paint an image that represents the feelings that the poem evokes. Let your intuition and breath guide you. After some time spent in sessions using the words and images from the book, experiment with writing a verse of your own that expresses your unique experiences, feelings, and understandings. Paint something that further expresses your words, in this moment. Read it again tomorrow and paint whatever that moment reveals. Remember, just as every moment is new and different than the one before, so is each painting. If you eventually move on from painting with water to painting with ink on paper—the traditional sumi-é (soo-me-ay) ink painting—remember the lessons learned from the fading images and continue to practice non-attachment and non-judgment.

The foremost aesthetic quality of Zen painting is that of profound simplicity. One image that embodies this aesthetic is the circle, or enso—a good image with which to start. The circle is a recurring symbol in Zen art that is created with a single brush stroke, in a single breath (you make the brush stroke as you exhale). It is simple, immediate, rhythmic, and naturally balanced—a few key characteristics of traditional Zen painting. The circle represents everything and nothing—or true enlightenment. It is said that one's inner balance and depth of realization is expressed and can be read in the *enso* that one paints. But do not get caught up in and concerned about the results. Simply concentrate on your practice and be in the process. Enjoy the moments of creation. Be aware of your breath, your hand, your eye, and your body—each moment. Let your painting be an extension of yourself and an expression of your inherent, inner nature. Paint with your breath and body, not with your thoughts. Nurture spontaneity. If you let your breath work for you, your painting will flow smoothly and naturally. And then with little effort your *enso*, and your mind, will be well balanced.

Breathe a full circle.

Let go of expectation;

And then—true nature.

MYOCHI

As fish dart through the water, they are forgetful of the water;
as birds fly on the breeze, they are not conscious that there is
a breeze. Discern this, and you can transcend the burden of
things and enjoy natural potential.

HUANCHU DAOREN

An enlightened being should develop a mind

that alights on nothing whatsoever.

THE *DIAMOND SUTRA*

Look lovingly on some object. Do not go on to another object.
Here, in the middle of this object—*the blessing.*

SHIVA

"Today I *am*" is the essential condition

and that is no other than the essence of Zen Buddhism.

EIDO ROSHI

Along this way

Goes no one.

Autumn evening.

BASHÓ

Snail at my feet—

Open space between two thoughts.

Where did you come from?

MYOCHI

The wind has settled, the blossoms have fallen;

Birds sing, the mountains grow dark—

This is the wondrous power of Buddhism.

RYOKAN

The hand sees, the eye

Draws, the body breathes.

Wake up! A rabbit.

MYOCHI

Day after day,

Day by day,

Dust of mind collects:

Be sure to wash it away

And find your original Self.

ZEN SAYING

The great Way has no gates:

There are thousands of different ways in.

ZEN PHRASE

Steadfastly doing nothing, sitting there
Spring comes and the grass grows of itself.

ZEN PHRASE

A wild goose

Passing the length of the sky

Casts a shadow

Into the cold water

The goose has no idea

Of leaving a trace,

The water no consciousness

Of the shadow sinking through.

ZEN PHRASE

Moonlight penetrates

To the bottom of the lake,

Yet no trace is left.

ZEN POEM

Does a dog have the Buddha-nature?

ZEN PHRASE

In the beginner's mind there are many possibilities;
In the expert's there are few.

SHUNRYU SUZUKI

Enlightened or not—

It is all the very same.

Have a cup of tea!

MYOCHI

When in worldly activity, keep attentive between the two breaths, and so practicing, in a few days *be born anew.*

SHIVA

The spring flowers, the autumn moon;

Summer breezes, winter snow.

If useless things do not clutter your mind,

You have the best days of your life.

MUMONKAN

The old pond,

A frog jumps in—

The water's sound.

BASHÓ

Without any intentional, fancy way of adjusting yourself,
to express yourself as you are is the most important thing.

SHUNRYU SUZUKI

Originally there's
No dust to sweep off:
The mind of the person
Who holds the broom is
Exactly like the dirt.

ZEN SAYING

Everything

Changes in this world

But flowers will open

Each spring

Just as usual.

ZEN POEM

We ought to listen to music

or sit and practice breathing

at the beginning of every meeting or discussion.

THICH NHAT HANH

It couldn't care less

Whose soil it may become:

Falling leaf.

ZEN POEM

Live in this moment.

The starry sky is just there—

Where else can you be?

MYOCHI

Think in this way of all this fleeting world:

As a star at dawn, a bubble in a stream;

A dewdrop, a flash of lightning in a summer cloud,

A flickering lamp, a phantom, and a dream.

THE *DIAMOND SUTRA*

SOURCES

Daoren, Huanchu. *Back to Beginnings: Reflections on the Tao.*
Translated by Thomas Cleary. Boston: Shambhala, 1990.

Hanh, Thich Nhat. *The Miracle of Mindfulness.* Boston: Beacon Press, 1975.

Lewis, Robert E., Zenrin Chidō, translator and editor. *Zen Grove Handbook.*
Jacksonville, FL: Zen Sangha Press, 2001.

Reps, Paul, compiler. *Zen Flesh, Zen Bones: A Collection of Zen and
Pre-Zen Writings.* Garden City, New York: Anchor Books, 1960.

Roshi, Eido Shimano. *Golden Wind: Zen Talks.* New York and Tokyo:
Japan Publications, Inc., 1979.

Sekida, Katsuki, translator (with commentary). *Two Zen Classics.*
New York and Tokyo: Weatherhill, Inc., 1977.

Shigematsu, Soiku, compiler and translator (with an introduction).
A Zen Harvest, Japanese Folk Zen Sayings. San Francisco: North
Point Press, 1988.

Stevens, John, translator. *Dewdrops on a Lotus Leaf: Zen Poems
of Ryokan.* Boston: Shambhala, 1993.

Suzuki, Shunryu. *Zen Mind, Beginner's Mind.* New York and Tokyo:
Weatherhill, 1970.

ABOUT THE AUTHOR

Myochi Nancy O'Hara was drawn to Zen Buddhism in the mid-1980s after the death of her father, and found solace in the profound stillness of silent meditation. In a Jukei ceremony in 1992, Nancy committed to the precepts of Buddhism and was given the Dharma name of *Myochi*, which means *Wondrous Wisdom.* All of her books, from *Find a Quiet Corner* to *Serenity in Motion,* offer spiritual guidance for everyday life based on the teachings of Buddhism. Nancy conducts meditation classes and workshops, and corporate seminars and retreats on mindfulness at work. She lives in New York City. Visit her at www.nancyohara.com.

ABOUT THE ILLUSTRATOR

Seiko Susan Morningstar was ordained as a Rinzai Zen Buddhist monk and studied at Dai Bosatsu Zendo Monastery under the guidance of Eido Tai Shimano Roshi and in Japan at Shogen ji Monastery with Sogen Yamakawa Roshi. She lives in New York City.